GETTING NAKED

WITH MY

CLOTHES ON

Understanding the Power
of Vulnerability

Jennifer King Brogan

ISBN: 978-1-7344756-0-9 (paperback)
ISBN: 978-1-7344756-2-3 (e-book)

What Women Are Saying About the Author

It feels like I've known Jennifer for decades when in fact we met just three years ago. Our relationship was divinely orchestrated bringing us together in a weekend of exploring women's leadership.

As providence would have it, our relationship quickly evolved into a partnership where we facilitated women's leadership together. It was one of the most seamless collaborations I've ever had.

What I have admired about Jennifer all along is her fierceness in the way she loves others and fights for people to overcome their own false limitations. She personally demonstrated a willingness to open herself up to all of the discomfort that comes with growth. I honor her for living what she teaches.

Jodi C Penrod
Transformational Leadership

***

Historically, I validated myself based on the many roles I played...daughter, wife, mother, grandmother, great grandmother, sister, nurse, friend. Jennifer challenged me to move out of my own way and question my ''I am'' She inspired me to step into my true identity and celebrate me.

By avoiding the negativity of self-talk, allowing herself to become vulnerable and expose herself from the inside out, Jennifer has inspired women from all walks of life to accept the true role of feminine grace.

Getting Naked With My Clothes On calls every women to experience vulnerability and be true to the powerful woman they were meant to be.

Wilma Albers, RN BSN
NurseConnect, LLC

***

"We all need someone to see us bigger then we see ourselves"

Jennifer King Brogan has been this someone for me. Jennifer has shifted the perspective I have had on my life for so long. She has shown me how to see my past as fuel for my future. She is an amazing woman with so many gifts. She is the real deal. Working with Jennifer has brought clarity to my purpose in life. She is teaching me how to not only be ok just where I am, but how to maximize each moment propelling me in to my calling.

Her wisdom is like no other! I have been able to open up and be raw, real, and dare I say it .vulnerable! She has taught me that when we are "surviving" we are not "thriving" I gain more insight into myself with each session we have.

She is a powerhouse and a gift to all who are willing to "Get Naked With Their Clothes On"

Aliyah V.,
Client, Mother, Survivor, Success Story

***

I met Jennifer in the Spring of 2017 at a personal development weekend retreat. I was initially intimidated by Jennifer. I'm not sure if it was her confidence, her height, her purple hair, or her beautiful RBF (lol) or a combination of all of it. I can tell you she has since grown into one of my strongest allies. In the time I have known her she has done everything I have heard her set her mind too. She pretty much knows the quickest way from Point A to Point B. She is loyal, kind, and determined. She has the talent of responding before reacting and is also trusting. She is a knowledge gatherer. As a small business owner, I have gone to Jennifer many times for advice on general business questions. I am so excited to see the release of this book and to witness to the next ideas that pop in her head. It's never boring, usually an adventure, and always for the greater good.

Nan Deason, President,
Deason Contracting & Installations

***

Jennifer is one of the most authentic and courageous women that I know. She has a special way of connecting with you where you feel heard & understood. I feel as if I have known her my entire life, when it has only been a couple of years.

Jenn is open, honest, vulnerable and committed to growth, others and her own. She provides a safe, non-judgmental space to be & discover yourself. As a strong and independent woman navigating in this world, I watch her balance her life and it's a gift to me. She is committed to empowering and supporting others, especially in seeking self-expansion. Jenn is an authentic, loving asset to the lives of others that is deeply valued by those whose lives she is a part. She is making a difference in this world through her many adventures and professional endeavors. Jenn is making a positive impact that will last generations. I am honored to call her my friend and follow her.

Choose you! Choose her! Choose growth!

Tammie Johnson,
Broker, Inspiring Real Estate

A Few Words from the Author

Scrunch... I told myself when I was younger that if I ever actually wrote a book that I would start a piece of it that way...Scrunch. Lol, it was the way my favorite book at the time started. The name of the book was "Just Gin" (close, right?). So, a hat's off to the author, Wallis Kendal, who made some type of impact on that younger me – I think it was that it was so outside the box from other books I had read that I identified – and I get to make good on what I told that younger Jenn.

I also want to take a moment to express my gratitude. I am who I am today because of my experiences and the people in my life. There are way to many to name each individually, though there are a few I feel I must.

To my mother, Wilma Albers, thank you for your courage and unconditional love. The world benefits even more with your voice being expressed.

To my daughter Jillian, you are the reason I was able to get myself out of bed many a day. Thank you for showing me what is really important in life.

To my daughter Kaitlyn, you are my greatest joy and deepest sorrow. You are as I am. Thank you for holding the mirror.

To my husband Tim, you are the epitome of the definition of the soulmate who arrives specifically to encourage development and growth to a higher state of consciousness. You challenge everything I think I know. Thank you for sharing this adventure with me. A deal's a deal.

To my grandson Alistair, you are the absolute light of my life. Your curiosity and imagination are other worldly. You are my "why". Thank you for letting me be your Nana. You give me reason to push to be better every day.

To my Grandma Sroufe, you were always my soft place to land. The one person that I knew, no matter what, would stand beside me. Thank you for showing me that while it is impossible to live up to the idealist version someone we love may have of us....it doesn't change the love. Looking forward to our next talk over a cup of coffee and a cigarette...and perhaps we'll split a cold biscuit.

I am beyond grateful to my friends who see me bigger than I see myself, who love and encourage me to be my authentic self. May I always return the level of friendship you have shared with me. I will never be the same because of you.

I am grateful to all the people who have trusted me enough to let me share my experience with them in an effort to let them see that they are not the sum of events or choices they have made previously, that they are worthy and the world needs them to find their purpose and shine their light. My life is forever changed from the experience.

Thank you to each of you on my launch team! This book would not be what it is without each of you and your invaluable feedback.

This book is written in interview style. It is intended to bring you, the reader, into the conversation in a way that allows you to feel a part of the conversation. I will share with you; I have had both positive and negative feedback about the style. I hope you enjoy it and find it inclusive. Either way, if you are so inclined, I would love to hear about your experience.

This book was transcribed from an interview I did with Subira Folami. A nod to her for what she is bringing to the world. I can attest that she had a positive impact on my life, and I look forward to seeing how she continues to positively impact the world around us.

This book is a peek into my life's journey and what I have come to know and believe. I hope you get to know me just a bit through the words on the pages and that it inspires you to want to know more. I believe that my journey has not been just for me, as I believe neither has yours been solely for you. As women, we share a bond that is untenable and often unspoken. We need one another. I am here to speak it out loud and tell each of you that **we matter, we are worthy, we each have a purpose** that can be fulfilled by no other, we are each an integral part of this **sisterhood of femininity**, that we are the **Creators**, that we are **Divine** and that each of us, no matter any labels that may have been stuck to us – even if we have previously accepted them- we are the epitome of **feminine grace**.

And lastly, please accept my heartfelt apology for any mistakes you find in the book. They do not represent a lack of passion for the work, I am just aware that perfection does not exist. At least not by the definition it has in this world right now,

Thank you for taking the time to read this book. I hope you get as much joy from it as I have gotten in preparing it to be shared with you.

From one Goddess to another,
Jennifer King Brogan

TABLE OF CONTENTS

"It isn't what I do, but how I do it. It isn't what I say, but how I say it, and how I look when I do it and say it."

- Mae West

Chapter 1

The Beginning (& 'Birthing' of Judge Judy)

Subira: "Hello everyone, I want to welcome you to Myths and Misconceptions about Vulnerability and Transformation. My name is Subira Folami.

In this episode of Myths and Misconceptions being recorded for broadcast today, I'm talking with the Creator of Envision Coaching© Co-Creator of Elevate!, addiction specialist, hypnotist, coach, motivational speaker and sustainable transformation expert Jennifer King Brogan, about the common myths and misconceptions surrounding the concepts of vulnerability and transformation that stop most women dead in their tracks, really, before they even summon the courage to move forward.

Welcome, Jennifer, I am so excited to have you here. Though, truth be told, I think I am even more excited for the women in the audience who will hear you today and reach out to engage with you on their journey. Whether it is through buying your book, attending your retreat, scheduling a coaching session or all the above. I think that when a woman chooses herself; it is a win for all.

Jennifer: "Subira, I couldn't agree with you more."

Subira: "Ok, there is so much to cover on this subject and especially with the insight that, Jennifer King Brogan, has to offer. So, to the audience a bit of background info, Jennifer is a well-known expert on the subject of vulnerability and the transformative experience, and she has graciously consented to this interview tonight. Her extensive knowledge and experience are such that we are looking to dispel some of the common myths and misconceptions in this area. We want to provide women, especially the over-40 crowd, an understanding of how embracing vulnerability is an empowerment move. It allows the possibility for it to be a catalyst for self-acceptance, transformation and creating an authentic life. That, Jennifer, is beautiful indeed."

Jennifer: "Thank you very much, Subira. I am honored to be here."

Subira: "This is so beautiful; I am actually anxious for this interview. I want to just jump right in. So, Jennifer, my first set of questions is going to be about your background and experience in the areas of vulnerability and transformation so that the women in our audience can really understand who you are, where you're coming from, and how you can relate to where they are right now in this very moment. After that what we'll do is we'll jump into the main areas where people have misunderstandings and misconceptions. We will look at vulnerability and we will look at transformation so that our audience can understand how to get past those limiting beliefs that often paralyze people even from getting started. Okay, so, tell us a little bit about yourself, Jennifer, in terms of your background, where you come from and some of your own life experiences."

Jennifer: "Oh my, I don't know how much time we have. I could talk on that so long it could be the only question you ask. (laughing)

Okay. Well. I grew up in a small town in Western Kansas. That ought to be far enough back for everyone. (laughing)

My dad was a farmer and my mom's a nurse. The town was small enough that everybody knew everybody. And everybody knew your business. Which gives you an idea, except, of course, not to leave out the important factor that if they didn't know your business, they made it up.

The community I grew up in was made up of mostly very, very traditional families living very conservative lifestyles. At least that was what they portrayed and the seat from which I felt judged. I didn't fit in very well from my perspective and was often reminded of the expectations that were placed upon me. Needless to say, that to everyone who held expectations for me, including myself, I failed to some degree or another. I believed that I was born defective and no matter what, I was damned if I do and damned if I don't. I didn't come to this belief overnight nor did I understand or succumb to it early or easily. It was fed to me throughout my life with the underlying message of being a huge disappointment to my family. Even more than being the offspring of a woman not fit for my father, I was supposed to be a boy, and to everyone's disgust and disappointment, I was a girl.

Now this information wasn't spoken directly to me, at least not the first few years. I received the information though, loud and clear. Originally, it was from my father's parents, my paternal grandparents. My granddad was very, very much the man runs the show and makes the decisions, the woman does what she's told and that is that. I remember a conversation when I was in high school on the topic of college educations – which was spurred by my youngest uncle's wife dropping out of college to support them so that he could complete his degree. I remember my grandfather saying, "Two years of college is enough for any woman." And as, I gave myself whiplash from whipping my head around so quickly in utter dismay and disgust, I said, "I suppose it is if you're settling for less than what you want. Assuming a degree is what you want." And yes, I was appalled at what I was learning about the family of my father and the baseline misogynistic belief systems that permeated not only the society I lived in but was being indoctrinated to my family. (heavy breath released) So that's what I grew up around on that side. I was a disappointment because I was supposed to be a boy, I was the oldest, the first born. And since I wasn't, there were certain rules and expectations I best live up to because I still carried the Sloan surname. Now, I also must acknowledge I had two girl cousins right around my age who did not have these same rules and expectations because they were my dad's nieces from his older sister, different last name you know. Nothing to point out that what they accomplished was really because of that side of their family...name and reputation to uphold ya know.

And mind you, I am certain you all caught this, my father's older sister, correct she was the oldest of five, my father second though oldest male child. Hypocritical, perhaps? I certainly thought so, though each of you can decide for yourself. Another little nugget for you, both of my father's sisters have four-year college degrees, of which, my grandfather made sure to boast every opportunity he had.

So, apparently, it was only if you were married to one of his son's, or he just deemed you less than or whatever, two years of college was enough. So, I grew up in this environment surrounded by judgment, misogyny and hypocrisy. Though, in the spirit of full disclosure, it wasn't much better on the maternal side. It was different so it made it more palatable apparently. Looking back, I would say it was like something disgusting dipped in chocolate, that on the outside appeared delicious and by the time you realized it wasn't, it was too late, you had already taken a big ol' bite. Blech! I digress. So, I played varsity ball, I was invited to play Junior Olympic basketball, I was Kansas Miss T.E.E.N. 1987, I just aged myself, oh well. I share those accomplishments, which were tip of the iceberg if you were to see the entire resume, because growing up, how I was brought up, was with the underlying theme that what is going on doesn't matter. Whatever the situation, unless it makes you or the family look good to everyone else, it just doesn't matter. What matters is how it looks to everyone else. What matters is only on the outside, what's happening inside or behind closed doors...not even relevant. To the degree of not even true!!! And don't you ever dare tell anyone anything different. So, as the consummate disappointment and innately defective daughter, I set out to prove my worth. Any guesses how that turned out? (laughing) Well, I became an overachieving, perfectionist with zero self-esteem as I had alluded to earlier and I learned quickly how to be a chameleon. I could adjust myself to fit into any group or situation based on other's words and behaviors.

"Millions of people live their entire lives without finding themselves. But it is something I must do."

- Marilyn Monroe

Chapter 2

The Chameleon Effect

And so, it went. I didn't feel like I fit in anywhere and I didn't feel like I belonged anywhere. Though I had this group of friends over here where I could be like this, then this group of friends over there where I could be like that, and never really, truly getting to understand or even really get to know the authentic nature of who I am.

I didn't even know what was up and what was down. Because it seemed like nothing was okay and everything was okay, and it was just, well, it was really kind of a nightmare to live and attempt to navigate alone without the information, skills or techniques to support such an endeavor. I quickly chose geographical relocation as a viable solution. I remember begging and pleading with my mom to move or to let me go live with some family members in another town. Of course, this didn't materialize though the fantasy of it kept me going. When I am able, I decided I wanted to graduate from high school early and go to college, so I did and right after I moved away, my father moved out.

So, backtracking a touch, I didn't mention that I have a younger brother. He is three and a half years younger than I am, and so he was still in school and living at home when I went away. It would have been the January of my senior year when I left. There were a series of events leading up to that decision, and I had had all that I was willing to withstand, so I just went ahead and went on to college, and it wasn't probably four weeks after that, that my dad picked up and left, and ... He left my mother during the bankruptcy they had filed jointly, so the house I grew up in was being sold, he had gone and bought a farmhouse out in the middle of nowhere and was having an affair with my mom's best friend. So he moved out to that farmhouse, he moved his mistress in – I say mistress, though as I hear it come out of my mouth it sounds way more glamorous than I think either of them deserve – apparently she really just wanted to kind of morph in there and take over my mom's life. It seemed to me that what she thought was that mom's life was quite amazing and I am here to tell you, it was not nearly as amazing as she thought it was. You could ask my mom that, however, she sure seemed to want to be mom. My mom had gotten her a job at the clinic where my Mom worked, and she was basically invited – or invited herself – to all the sporting events we attended. Every time I turned around POOF! there she was! So was all this craziness and chaos she brought with her. Very single, white female-ish, and I remember during this timeframe, before we knew of the affair, I told Mom, I said, "Look, I don't like her. I don't trust her. I know you say she's your friend and whatever... I want nothing to do with her. Just keep her away from me! I have no hard evidence to explain, except there's something about her that I find shady and uncomfortable to be around."

That was one of the first times I remember ever voicing my intuition and standing on it, because that really was not an acceptable thing in my family either. Let alone have an opinion, if it was different than anybody else's, especially my father's or grandfather's, heaven forbid.

I think that I have felt the innate desire to speak my truth from a young age and was very aware that I was not to do so. In my mind it didn't matter anyway, I was defective just by the very nature of who I am. It created a very difficult situation as a child, especially as a teenage girl growing up, because my dad and I had an 'ok on the surface' relationship until...well, until I hit puberty and then I guess he didn't know what the hell he was supposed to do with that and we would argue, and we would fight and it was a standoff of wills... And at the end of the day, all I really wanted was... for him to love me and for him to be proud of me, for me to be good enough just the way I was. The only time I remember him telling me he was proud of me was when I got to start at the District and State basketball tournaments, as a sophomore. It's kind of a Friday Night Lights sort of thing, though with basketball instead of football. It was that way where I grew up... So, it's kind of a big deal. My dad was an athlete too, he played college basketball. I just remember when the game was getting ready to start and Coach Brown came over to me when the whistle blew for the starters to be introduced and he told me to get my warmups off, I was starting. I remember the butterflies and the excitement I felt, just like it was yesterday. I remember looking up into the stands to find my dad and to see if he knew. I could tell that he had no prior knowledge of coach's decision because as I saw the look of understanding of what was taking place, I saw his smile broaden, his chest swell and I swear that man was floating about five inches above the ground.

It still makes me smile to think of it. Then it fades just as quickly,

because what I also remember was when I was Kansas Miss T.E.E.N. and him yelling and screaming at my mom about all of the money that was spent on this, that and the other, how spoiled I was, how much time this shit took, etc. and on one of the days he was on a tirade about all this, I had an event that was being put on by a local organization. The Colby Diplomats, I believe, of which my Grandma Sroufe, mom's mom, was one – no need to spell all that out to you, I'm sure - So I was there and I was doing my thing, I was going to be performing my talent, modeling my evening gowns, and speaking to the room prior to my leaving for the National pageant. I was in the back waiting to be introduced, when much to my surprise my dad got up in front of everyone and talked about what an amazing experience this is for our family, and how proud we are of Jennifer, etc., etc. And once again, I am dumbfounded at the hypocritical bullshit coming out of his mouth. At home it is a topic of contention, in public it is an honor and an amazing experience. Now, with some time passing and some life experience having occurred, I can look back and realize it was what he knew and was willing to accept, apparently without question, yet that changes nothing for the seventeen-year-old me listening to it. At least I didn't subscribe to that "don't question, just do what you're told" kind of thinking. Though I am sure there are some people who are or were in my life that wish I had at least tested the theory.

Anyway, it was just those kind of things over and over and over that I was just like, "I don't understand, and yet I can see where, if I pretend to be this it serves me here and if I pretend to be this it serves me there and not necessarily understanding how or why... because underneath all of that, I believed I was defective. The entire time I didn't even realize most of that underlying limiting belief system I was following even existed. I got to that awareness later in my life after doing some of this work. It was such a realization that I made all these decisions in my life based on the fact that I thought I was damned if I do and damned if I don't, because there is absolutely no way that I can turn myself into an actual first born son for him. So, I was always going to be a disappointment.

Subira: "So, I'm hearing you say, basically you splintered.... yourself, and I don't know, would it be accurate to say you kind of felt a little chaotic? And this might be an extreme word, but... And I'm not using it medically, I'm just...honestly, my imagination says that probably feels a little like schizophrenia sounds like it might... Oh, I'm here on this, then over here, and then I'm over there, then over here and there, I'm all of these and none of these, shwoo...

You know a lot of chaos all the time, in your mind."

Jennifer: "Actually, I used to somewhat jokingly say– prior to my understanding of and working in the mental health field of course - I'm having a Sybil moment. Attempting to make as light of it as possible and it was about the only way I could describe it or that I could relate it to so that someone might understand it. I...so it's very... It's very disheartening, and to top it off I also became a perfectionist.

Subira: "You had learned to read cues from people in authority. The most subtle cues about... Oh, that cue, when I see that on that person, that means I'm doing good. It's kind of like you're learning to play. What is that game? We play it as kids.

Red light, green light or hot & cold or whatever and you're like, "Am I moving in the right direction of... Oh! I'm getting cold. Okay, let me go over here, okay? Now, I'm getting warm." Was it kind of like that? Is that even a bit close at all?"

.

"Freedom's just another word for

nothing left to lose."

- Janis Joplin

Chapter 3
The Flip Side

Jennifer: "That was kind of how it was. Some of that and it even got to the point where I was just like, Nope! Done. I just became hugely defiant and I was...so angry. I felt like I had been lied to and duped. Everything you have taught me is bullshit. I have no idea who I am or what I believe. My entire foundation crumbled. And now you aren't holding up your end of the deal. I felt like everything I thought I knew and every choice I had made was a lie. I was like, "It doesn't matter what I do, I have done all of these things and it still isn't enough! Everything I had thought and believed about myself, other people, the world...was ripped to shreds and I had no idea what to do. So, I went from one extreme to the other. "Follow the rules and perform girl" with that drive to be perfect and there was "Go fuck yourself girl" that was the flip side and I could certainly swing from one end of that pendulum to the other!

I have since learned that perfectionism is one of the walls we put up when we don't feel worthy, when we don't have that understanding of self and on top of that, in my case, you have been taught that what is happening on the inside doesn't matter but you damn well better look good on the outside! So, living in that enviromnent, to be vulnerable is to be weak. So, what did I do? I put my worth in the unattainable expectation of being perfect, because if I do it perfectly; you can't judge me. When underneath the jury had voted, the judge had banged the gavel and anything else that was said was only more evidence for stricter sentencing.

Oh, do I love her now though. That Jennifer the one who while harshly judging herself so she didn't have to practice the art of being vulnerable, the one who believed that she was defective and was afraid if she let you in you would have proof of the same, that Jennifer is tough. She is tough and smart and brave. She kept me alive and moving forward. She even allowed for me to create some amazing things in my life through that time, partially because of the misguided beliefs. So, there is always two sides, and all comes to a full circle...we're just not to that part of the journey just yet.

So, not too long after my mom and grandma came to tell me about dad leaving and the pending divorce, my dad came to my dorm at college. I had come back to the dorm and walked into the lobby on a Wednesday, I believe. A bunch of us were all going to get ready to go out and do something. Something, ha, I just casually say that as if it was so benign or that I don't recall...we were all going to the bar. Of which, mind you, anyone could determine the night of the week by which bar we could be found at, so I know that I had placed myself in situations where I was ripe to choose a solution that did not lend to the long-term results I wanted to achieve, hell of an effective short-term solution though!

Anyway, my dad is standing there in the lobby and I'm like, "Oh okay, and he's like... I just wanted to talk to you for a minute...Okay, so in my head I'm thinking, is it possible that this could allow for communication?... So, he takes me to his truck...We go to grab something to drink. We got a soda and we're sitting there talking in his truck, and I told him, I said, "Dad you know grandma, grandpa their lifestyle was how you were brought up. Grandpa makes all the decisions and "Grandma does whatever he told her to do. That was the model that you had, that's what you saw!"

And then you guys are over here, you and mom over here, you're telling me I can do anything I want to do; I can be whatever I want to be and it's the sky's the limit.

And Mom is caught in between. Being brought up with these certain roles, things that you do and don't do, and from your perspective it looks so different. And then she's also like... Wait a minute, I want to do what I want to do as well. I have hopes and dreams. Why am I expected to follow the old model? Because one of the big fights that they had, I specifically recall, was when my Mom went back to school to become a nurse. She had quit school, quit college because she got pregnant with me, and then she helped put my dad through college. So, my dad had the degree, and Mom didn't, and I had even heard him say that one of his instructors used to tell him to tell his wife she wrote an excellent paper! My grandfather, paternal, was also involved in this discussion/argument, my guess is they were borrowing the money for her to go back from him which created one helluva power differential for sure. Mom stood her ground on this one. I just remember promising myself that I would never let this happen to me. I was never going to have my life determined by a man. Any man! So, that's where that storyline in my life began – at least to the best of my recollection – and it was reinforced often. Anyway, back to our conversation in his truck. I said to him, "You know what, since I'm out of the house maybe you and mom won't argue so much. 'Cause they always argued about me. All the time. So, here's his response, he goes, "Well you know what, maybe you're right. Maybe since you're gone it will be easier. Knowing the whole damn time, he was already having an affair. Already knowing that he had no intention of working on anything with my mother and he couldn't even take responsibility for his own shit... even then. Heaven forbid he ever tell the truth! Oh no, he always chooses to take the easier for him in the moment way. No consideration at all for anyone else, let alone his own daughter. I was like, fuck, well, okay, okay, yeah, let yourself get duped into thinking perhaps it could be different, nice job, Jennifer. So that exchange and our further encounters, added to the other beliefs I had because I wasn't a boy and how I was never going to give a man that kind of power in my life; I decided that since dad's don't act like that, dad's don't desert their daughters – especially not ones who had accomplished everything I had accomplished in so few years – so the only logical conclusion to which I could come was, yep, you got it...I am defective, there is something inherently wrong with me, when everyone else finds out that my own father didn't even love me they wouldn't either & they would leave because that's what men do. So here I am, damned if I do and damned if I don't – reinforcing that belief I started into back in the second grade; thank you Mrs. Taylor. And then began my less than industrious drinking and drugging career. So, that was the beginning of college, what bits of it I went to, and I continued to turn to drugs and booze to escape myself and for a long time it worked. That is what many people, even in the addiction treatment industry fail to acknowledge... drugs and alcohol are absolutely viable solutions that work. May not be the most effective to reach other desired results, though they work. I digress, I ended up getting into a bit of legal trouble. Thankfully, it ended up being very minimal. It's not even on my record. However, it could have been much, much worse. It was enough I was extradited to another state! Now there's a story for you. I'll save that one for another day. I finally decided that my solution du jour was no longer working and had in fact begun contributing to my challenges. Though that realization didn't even take hold with me enough to even address it until I was 35. And that was just addressing my no longer effective solution; the drugs and alcohol. Those substances were not what needed addressing for actual transformation— it was my perspective of myself, other people and the world."

Subira: "Well, let me ask you this, when did you become aware that way, that your current way of being and doing, the choices you had made and were making, the results you were creating, that they weren't working for you?"

Jennifer: "First, before I answer that, please let me clarify what I just said of the drugs and alcohol not being what needed to be addressed. They needed to be addressed in that I needed to not continue utilizing them. Though what would ultimately lead to transformation was not that and that alone. Now to your question, I think that several times along the way through the journey of this life, that I knew that my choices and what I was doing wasn't sitting well with my spirit, that they weren't aligning with that part of me that was connected, that was still seeking its purpose. And I was also not comfortable with the shame and self-judgment that was my life, so the cycle continued and spiraled because they do work.

I had such deeply rooted limiting beliefs and strong subconscious programming, just like we all do, that I was only able to do what I was able to do. Which for quite some time was what I'd always done... Not because of lack of ability, because I just didn't know what I didn't know.

"Everywhere, even in the blackest abyss, he believed one might witness the divine. The shadows and contrast—absence itself—as important as the light and marble, for one cannot exist without the other."

- Eowyn Ivey, <u>To The Bright Edge of the World</u>

Chapter 4
The Yin Yang Principle

Thinking about that part of my journey makes me think of Maya Angelou, when she said, "Do the best you can until you know better. Then when you know better, you do better."

Subira: "Yeah, that is one of my favorites."

Jennifer: "Mine too. I do believe in the goodness in people. I also believe in the darkness in people, for lack of a better word. I truly believe that for myself and everyone else. I also believe I must accept that both are real in order to reach an understanding of this journey of being human.

We, human beings, are capable of many, many things and not all of them would be labeled positive by our society's standards. I must acknowledge and hopefully accept that I and all humanity is capable of a gamut of behaviors. If I don't, then I am resisting a part of myself... and when you resist, what you resist will

,sist. This is key to self-acceptance and true ₂mpowerment. I believe that so strongly that during my Women's Empowerment Retreat, called Elevate Her! the curriculum contains exercises that allow women to come in touch with what that really means, in a safe, nonjudgmental space because it's powerful to acknowledge that both exist. Then, if you accept both, without judgment, and embrace your wholeness they become available to you in any situation because then you can choose. You can choose whether you want to have a response this way or a response that way. When you don't acknowledge all of you and embrace it, and this applies to all of humanity, then it starts controlling you, you will start reacting from places that you don't want to because you're not acknowledging and owning that they are part of who you are, denying your wholeness. It is interesting to observe people and their judgments of this embracement of duality. I have, now I don't want to scare anybody who's listening, but I often illustrate my point intensely, and have told people that when you see me coming toward you, please know that while I am absolutely capable of throwing my arms around you and hugging you tightly...I am also capable of walking right up to you and wrapping my hands around your throat instead. Both of those "Jennifer's" are in here and available to me in whatever situation may arise.

I say that in an effort to help illustrate that all of that is within each of us. It must exist this way for without one there is not the other. Life is not all sunshine and glitter all the time and most importantly - that's not what love means. Love doesn't always mean I'm gonna tell you what you wanna hear or we're always gonna be happy and there's gonna be rainbows and unicorns and we never argue, and we agree on everything. First of all - boring. Second - totally dishonest - and the "I love you enough to tell you the truth kind of love" is sharing the hard things. It's like saying, "Hey you know what, this is not okay, and I am not going to allow you to treat me in that manner. My boundary is this and I am not willing to change it to be with you and I will not volunteer to be treated in such a manner." It is the ability to give and receive feedback as a gift, even though most of society is opposed and it can be super uncomfortable.

It's the ability to take a stand for something that you believe in and sometimes you turn around and you're standing alone, and it can be lonely and still worth it... You get to choose if you own all of that. So, you get to see where love comes from in different ways in different spaces, and then you get to know that you can play different because you're not being controlled by one side or the other one that you have denied. I know people who deny they have a good side, that light side of them, because it's too uncomfortable because they're limiting beliefs and their subconscious thoughts are telling them they're bad, you're defective, you're not enough, those kinds of things. And so, for them acknowledging the light, the love, the good, the caring is just as painful as it is for people who have the opposite that don't want to acknowledge that there can be a "dark" side to them. You know what though, personally, I would much rather pull out my darkside girl, if someone were coming to hurt my child than be the one that's like, in a Suzy Sunshine way "Hey, I really don't think this is a good idea and I am asking you nicely not to hurt us, blah, blah... That's not effective from my perspective. I say embrace and respect them both because it is part of humanity, it's who we are, the duality is necessary for the existence of either."

Subira: "I love that about especially that respect of light and dark, I think for great illustration is Star Wars, you have the light and the dark and that whole movie, that whole franchise, is about that battle to embrace that Luke Skywalker was from The Dark."

Jennifer; "Yes, it is a classic theme. Because on whatever level people are willing to admit it, we all fight the battle within."

Subira: "And if you think about it, honestly, we all are born, we're actually created in darkness. The womb... is dark, there's no light in the womb.

Jennifer: "That's true. Much is created in the dark actually."

Subira: "So sometimes, especially in the personal development spiritual world, there's all this, like you said, I love rainbows, and unicorns, and glitter, and not acknowledging, and there is also a lot of power, in dark but you have to be what you said, "respect it, honor it, acknowledge it," all that stuff. I think that what you said was so, so powerful."

Jennifer: "Thank you. It also... well, it serves in a lot of areas. The acknowledgement of the duality is paramount. A portion of my professional work with people who have drug challenges and have become involved in the criminal justice system express they feel judged and basically considered throw away members of society, or definitely unwanted by most of the rest of society. I have been told by so many of them that I am the only person who has ever sat with them and said, "I believe in you, and I will be here with you and we'll do this. It's that whole walking through someone else's darkness. Pema Chödrön has my favorite definition of compassion. What she said, and I quote, I'm pretty sure I got this one;

"Compassion is not a relationship between the healer and the wounded, it's a relationship between equals. Only when we know our own darkness well can we be present with the darkness of others. Compassion becomes real when we recognize our shared humanity."

Acknowledge, accept, embrace...embrace it all. It is the only way to be whole, to live from love and compassion, to live your purpose, to be the difference you want to see in this world and it must come from that love and compassion - not judgment. Denial of any of yourself is judgment and creates a chasm in your relationship with your own Divinity which in turn separates you from others."

"I just want everyone to please just practice this."

Subira: "I mean that's... She's one of my favorites too."

Jennifer: "Yes, wise words."

"All of life is a constant education."

- Eleanor Roosevelt

Chapter 5

The Human Journey Is the School of Hard Knocks

Subira: "So let me ask you this, have you had formal training or education where it comes to vulnerability, and transformation or have you learned it just kind of the school of hard knocks of life?"

Jennifer: "I think I have the best of both worlds. I definitely have a degree from the School of Hard Knocks... But that's the human journey. We all get to have that. It just looks different for each person. And then I have done work for myself to be able to recognize and deal with some of my own darkness, so to speak. It's really that subconscious programming that we all have. That script that tells you who you're 'supposed' to be that is the professor in many areas of life. Actually, more dictator/protector, less educator/supporter. Especially if your experience is feeling that you have been "cast" into the wrong role, perhaps even the wrong play or show. I know for myself, I at times envision the closing credits and I will have many roles in front of my name. One I for sure played was "Girl with Daddy Issues". I am not making light of anyone's journey. I just know that I am prone to take myself too seriously and separate from others. Truly, when you have worked through your stuff it can often become quite amusing in hindsight.

Then by way of formal education, my degree is in Human Services, which I translated into my career in the field of addiction. I'm a board-certified clinical supervisor and a certified hypnotist and coach. Having complementary skill sets has allowed me to be able to create and implement enhanced support tools and techniques.

I have training in several modalities of therapy. I began this when I returned to college after I decided that perhaps drug use, no matter how effective a solution for numbing myself, wasn't the answer for me. Drugs are a super effective way to change one's feelings instantaneously, as well as allowing forgetfulness to anything or everything. Though for me, I wasn't able to also create the life I dreamed while I was numbing myself. I had to really take a good hard look at and into myself, accept what was completely and then begin being the woman who was able to create the life she desired. This is still my journey.

I worked for a treatment facility while I was in school and several years after. When my experience of and working with our population of clients who were having challenges and unwanted consequences related to their substance use and my vision moving forward was drastically different than the organization where I was employed, I quit. There was more to it from a personal perspective as I was supervised by a misogynist and I was working in a rural community which has its own set of "rules" to play by if you want to even be allowed to play, so to speak. So, I had my own lessons through all this, however, when there were unethical demands, I took a risk and started an agency in the same community.

My team and I work with the adult alternative treatment court model, Drug Court, as it is affectionately known. My passion for over the last decade had been focused in this arena and it served me, my clients and the community well.

However, it is the alternative treatment court, because it is helping people that have substance use challenges and have become involved in the criminal justice system. They participants may not all have drug charges. They may have committed a crime, such as burglary, car theft, assault, etc. However, it all stems from their drug usage, and lack of other skills to be able to live differently. It goes right back to you don't know what you don't know and then when you know better than you can do better. Just as Maya Angelou would say. It also has so much to do with so many other factors, e.g. trauma, education level, income level, family, mental health issues, etc., etc. and the lack of education and understanding in certain pieces of the model have left too much room for opinion or personality for my comfort level. Though, it is still I higher quality of care for that set of circumstances and has been approved and made available in almost all areas. More so, than any other I know of that is as widely accepted.

I created my hypnosis focused business, aptly named, the Holistic Freedom Group... as I'm sure you can see the theme forming. I have been witness to the freedom that has been obtained for so, so many from all walks of life, I wanted to honor it. Freedom and liberty are my personal mantra.

I've also been working with Dr. Adi Jaffe and his IGNTD! recovery program. We have like-minded belief systems when it comes to addictions and working with people. I won't take up your time telling the story of how this came though it could be considered "crazy". However, there is no doubt in my mind that this connection was meant to happen. If anyone is familiar with Universal Laws, I guarantee this was an energetic collaboration.

I'm thrilled to be involved with IGNTD! and I'm also super excited about my new transformative coaching and individual/team development and empowerment company, called Elevate! It is the brainchild of myself and my long-term friend and now business partner, Dave Canoy. Elevate! also ties to my newest empowerment program, Envision Coaching, where I meld my different skills, tools, experience, talent and expertise into a progressive program of transformation with sustainable change.

Subira: "Well, I think it's so beautiful, how everything you've done has been a part of the puzzle and how it's all just so beautifully coming together."

Jennifer: "And I would never have thought such a thing when I was arguing with my dad, or he kicked me or I was in college and you knew what day of the week it was, by which bar we were at or any of the many challenging events in my life. All those events that just seem so debilitating and final... and they are life altering, they really are. However, what I have come to know and embrace, is that those things all happened FOR me. They absolutely happened for me to be able to then utilize those lessons to find my purpose and to help other people."

Subira: "Yeah, they were... Like you were raw material, the unmolded clay."

Jennifer: "Absolutely, I absolutely was. I just did not realize how much of the sculptor I also was."

Subira: "So tell us what kind of things you've done or experienced you had again within this whole space of vulnerability and transformation that are relevant to the audience that you're speaking to right now specifically where it comes to connection and women being socialized to suppress their true life purpose, their voice, and their vision. That's a big one. I know that's a big question, but I know you got a big answer for us."

Jennifer: "Oh, it actually it's huge. And that one in particular, that concept is actually near and dear to my heart because that whole growing up thinking that because I was a female that I was defective led me to, well, I'm also six-foot-tall, so I am very... let's just say I was not the sought after chick in Junior High. Let me tell you the boys were 4 foot 2 and I was already 5 foot 10 by the eighth grade. It just reinforced those limiting beliefs and was not working in my favor at that time.

I was athletic, and that kind of height did work for me there. That was where my relatively short-lived basketball career began. I had actually wanted to be a cheerleader. The girl's high school basketball coach apparently had different ideas and was overheard suggesting just that to the school sponsor of the cheerleading squad. Small towns...already a resentment would just continue to build.

I took on many attributes of male thinking because that was what I had been raised and conditioned to do on some level. I would be the one that I would defend my little brother. I would be the one that was expected to go to the farm and work with my dad, Jeff would stay and do whatever. The son he actually did have did not have those expectations put on him. I have no idea what the thought process was there. I likely never will.

I'm very direct, which can be uncomfortable for so many no matter the gender, though coming from a woman it often triggers a reaction. I'm at times aggressive, honestly, at that point in time, way more aggressive than I choose today. I've learned about choosing between aggressive and assertive because both can serve depending on the situation. However, I probably over did some of it out of a defense mechanism from not being enough, because I'm a woman, and I took on just about anything that was in front of me to take on. Quite honestly, I was really, really successful at almost everything and I was still really, really miserable. Because first of all, no matter what I did, it wasn't gonna change anything.

And being able to understand then that gender stuff was not about me, that it belonged to my dad and his dad and whomever. It was also very interesting because my mom was very much like, she wanted to dress me up and she wanted to have this pretty little angel that looked and acted so perfect – because that of course would mean she must be a very good mother... So, I was like learning to navigate these really conflicting expectations and there I am in the middle going - What in the hell is happening? I don't even know what to do."

Subira: "So, you were in a very unusual situation for a kid I would think."

Jennifer: "Oh, I felt I was... I absolutely felt I had to navigate this alone because I had already learned we don't ask for help...that makes us weak. We don't let anyone know what is truly happening it must always look good on the outside. And of course, my contribution to that internal dialogue was, don't let anyone know that you are defective and that you are damned if you do and damned if you don't. Because if anyone else knows, then the jig is up, you're done, you will never be able to have a life worth living. Then I would decide, ok, this is who I am, and I would go to school for that, or I would go do a job like I was a paralegal, I was gonna be an attorney. I was sure that was the direction and then that I don't even remember why I forget really, however all of those things would get side railed because it didn't have anything to do with who I am, it had to do with what can I put on to make it okay for everybody else so that they will just leave me alone because it's not about knowing who you are anyway. And to have the kind of drive I had, yet not believe that it could be real for me. It was real for everyone else, whatever that was. Now I believe that it is our spirit, that connected part of us that pulls us toward that who we are and why we're here. We are all here for different purposes and ultimately for one in the same. We each have a unique purpose within the larger purpose and there's a part of us that realizes, if we get in tune with it, that we must follow that siren's song of sorts, when we first become aware that it's there and that we must follow it and be able to express it in the world. It often seems more like a curse than a blessing when you are also attempting to navigate all of this in the world. Though when the understanding of its origin comes to light and you know it's not a true siren's song but a connection to the Divine. You are the embodiment of the Divine feminine. So then it's even more confusing because women are socialized to believe that the truth for them is the kids come first, and the husband comes before them, it is absolutely unacceptable to not have a husband or kids either because you must, as if it's your duty by being born female, which also means you must prescribe to the current definition of "beautiful" or you are basically useless. Oh no, you're not getting off the proverbial hook that easy, so while you do all that, you're also going to run this company from behind the male figurehead at likely half his salary and you're going to be the room mother and president of the PTA because it fills in some of that "spare time" you are always hearing about and if there's anything that's off-track in any of it well then, you're not a good enough and that is just not acceptable. What is wrong with you? Oh, before you answer that you must remember you must do all of that while acting like a lady while being very Emily Post about it, be seen and not heard when it's expected and all of that absolutely ridiculous crap."

"Maybe the princess could save herself. That sounds like a pretty good story too."

- Marissa Meyer

Chapter 6
Amazon Princess

Subira: "Yes, yes, yes. So, tell me this, talk to me about these two words that are really powerful. And then when you put them together, it's like boom. And that is the divine feminine. I would love to hear your understanding, experience of the divine feminine, especially from a woman who's six foot tall."

Jennifer: "Right, right, I do believe Wonder Woman was an Amazon. We are pretty awesome. I'm going to own that one right now, because let me tell you, I probably would have been bawling if somebody had called me that in public when I was younger. Well, I know that they used to call me an Amazon, and it was meant and received as an insult ... Right now, I'll own that internal Amazon, my Wonder Woman. Interesting enough right now is that you focused on the Divine Feminine which the Divine Feminine has been such an amazing revelation and relationship for me. So much so that there is a specific experience that is a transformational benchmark moment for the women involved in the women's empowerment weekend, that without giving it away, changes the perspective of 'woman' and the meaning of being a woman as well.

It is an exercise that's purpose is so important... Because the truth from my perspective, my truth is that, as women, we are the creators. We are the creators upon which this amazing, joyful and heart-wrenching responsibility has been bestowed... We birth life, we create what is here and then we nurture it and hold it together as it develops and expands and usually nowadays, we're dancing backwards in our heels as we do it. However, from a Divine Mother perspective, we have the most important space that anyone could have. That is so, just so huge ... And for me to come to understand the power in that...it holds the key to so much understanding. For me, in this journey of love and acceptance of self, that understanding, that definition of feminine that is not what I internalized from my childhood, the one that makes feminine synonymous with weak, broken, less than. It gave me understanding and permission to show up differently. That in all truth, feminine is the exact opposite of all that. Feminine is strong, nurturing, abundant and the power of feminine can be bold and in your face, it also doesn't have to be loud, doesn't have to be abrasive, it doesn't have to be from a competitive space, though it can be.

And women very much own that space and it's beautiful, it's absolutely beautiful. I own that space. I know that I personally bought for a long time that old definition and became the embodiment of what I had been told I was supposed to be and wasn't so I would always fall short, but absolutely don't be weak. And let me tell you, I fought that for a very, very long time. Some days I still do."

Subira: "I don't know if you're aware of it, but wherever that question came from - when you started speaking on that - everything about you in that split second, like you went somewhere, that was really... is really beautiful."

Jennifer: "Thank you. Yeah, it's something I get really emotional talking about it, just simply because I denied that part of me for so long and judged it harshly. So much so that I requested to often only work with male clients during part of my career. Now, I have a partner who does the men's version of my women's retreat, though my experience lay with the ability to be effective with either gender separately and people who knew this was the direction I was going had said to me while we were in the planning stages that, Jenn, you know all that stuff, you can teach it to the guys. They relate to you. And I thought to myself that, well, of course, they do. I spent most of a lifetime researching just that. However, I said while that may be true, I am not going to be facilitating the men only portion. I didn't say no because I wasn't capable, I said no because I don't want to do that. I want to honor the feminine in me and in these women that I'm so blessed to work with and I'm not gonna do it. I am simply no longer willing. And if that had meant we were unable to have a retreat for men initially, then we wouldn't have it. Thankfully, not the case, though very real for me to choose that position."

Subira: "Wow, that's beautiful, that's just, wow.

"I believe that you have to walk through vulnerability to get to courage, therefore . . . embrace the suck."

- Brenè Brown

CHAPTER 7
EMBRACE THE SUCK

Subira: "Alright, well, so tell me this. You have accomplished a lot, you have accomplished so much, you express yourself in your life, in so many different ways, so many different aspects of yourself and you've had a lot of success. Especially when you look at the whole spectrum, the whole continuum of your life that you have lived to this point. And so, I'd like to know if you feel like one night, well just like the light bulb went off and it was like, boom, I get it.

Or was it more of an unfolding, gradual even to sometimes I gotta be down on my forearms, crawling, working for it, kind of experience?"

Jennifer: "Oh, the idea of this work being learned overnight or an epiphany, I wish. And I really don't, because it was all of the experience that fueled my growth. And the idea is I choose, I had to choose to dive in 'cause I'm telling you what, I'll be right up front, if anybody tells you that working on yourself personally and personal transformation is not a journey in uncomfortable.

Don't, just don't... Go somewhere else because that's not true, it is very, well it is uncomfortable and it must be, it must be uncomfortable. It's the only way to shake that up for you to be able to then really start moving. So no, I definitely had claw marks on some stuff that I didn't want to let go of, for sure. And there is often, "Oh boy, are you serious? I'm going to have to do the belly crawl to get from here to there? I don't know how. I'm not strong enough. And fighting through that and doing it anyway. It is worth every uncomfortable moment of it. However, it's what I still have ongoing. Actually, I guess we can talk about different measures of success or how we want to define it though, what I truly believe is that this is a life-long learning commitment to myself.

And for me to honor myself, this person that I am here for this experience, is that it's my commitment, truly my covenant, that, with my understanding of the Divine, is to do this work, continue to do it for myself, and I can, I know that I can grow in any... any area. Which from a psychological and/or sociological perspective is super fascinating to me because I was quite judgmental.

Coming here from where I grew up versus, my understanding of today is this.... Don't prejudge. I can learn something from anyone, in any experience, at any time, whether they've done this work, or whether they are brand new walking in the door and just say something that is like... Oh, oh, oh, you said that, for me, That didn't have a thing to do with you honey. So that's what I think, I think it's a lifelong learning commitment. Because the deal is this – our journey here is all about relationships – about connection – about being of service to others – it is all about love. Love in its many forms. Love is always the answer. Always."

Subira: "Well, what I can tell you is that it's obvious that you are the right expert for us when it comes to personal development, vulnerability and transformation. I think what I'd like to do now is take us down the road and look at those myths and misconceptions and let's clear those up for people that are listening."

"Let go of who you think you're supposed to be; embrace who you are."

\- Brenè Brown

CHAPTER 8

FUCK IT! SOMETIMES YOU GOTTA LET 'EM SEE YA SWEAT

Subira: "What is the most common myth or misconception that women have about vulnerability?"

Jennifer: "I would say that in my experience the most common is that vulnerable is synonymous with weak, that it shows weakness for sure. My personal relationship with vulnerable was definitely that because coming from a masculine type of energy that says, 'Stand up and get in their face' and 'Don't you let them see you sweat, let alone cry!"

However, what it really converts into for myself and from the women I've worked with is - I'm afraid I'm gonna get hurt, so I'm not gonna open up. You're gonna use anything I may share with you against me.

Then my vulnerability and my openness become a weapon, and it's scary, it's really scary. I'm a true believer we do things based on love or fear and if I'm not doing something out of love and I need to see inside or underneath then I'm like... Okay, wait a minute, what am I afraid of? What is this that is underlying... And the stuff that's happening and it's uncomfortable because I'll tell you the other thing is that not all women are kind to one another. Did you know that?

Subira: "Yeah, unfortunately yes."

Jennifer: "I know, I know it is real for most. So much so we address it through an exercise called, "Why don't you trust women?"

We're conditioned to that though, we are conditioned that we are taught she's sneaky, she's underhanded, she wants him or her or whatever. And so, we are brought up with, don't get close, don't let her in... And so, the same person that has the same attributes that I have, I have to keep them at a distance; because I have to keep myself safe; even on a subconscious level. And the truth is, all we all want is connection. So, when I am not trusting you - I am not trusting me."

Subira: "Right. And I will tell you, I'm Your Midwest sister.

Subira: "My dad side from Missouri, from St. Louis and all that and my mother's side being from Kansas City, Kansas. And my experience is that the women that I grew up with and around from the Midwest are... We were raised in a way just to kind of, I don't know if 'hard' is the right word... but definitely tough. I mean, like you said, farmers... And if it needs to be done, it needs to be done. It's all hands-on deck. And I don't care how you feel like this needs to be done.

Jennifer: "Yes, feelings were not relevant, right?

Subira: "Is that sense of vulnerability and softness even in women who did have the luxury of showing up soft; still have the sweat of the brow kind of plow through... I know this, at least in my experience or the women that I grew up with and around, in Kansas and Missouri, there's a certain work ethic that's real. Like we got a toughness to us that can really squash that divine feminine and being willing to go through the break down that happens when you are transforming.

Jennifer: "Absolutely."

Subira: "The surrendering."

Jennifer: "There's something about that mid-western culture that is very much... We're hard-working. That's one of the things that, that is a thing of pride for Midwest. My family does what I do. We bring them along, they all participate. And at one point in time, I think as far as evolutionary-wise, when it was the dust bowl era or times of war and when they were out, and it was just the farming and all that that was necessary for survival. It became such a status thing for... We're all hard-working, we don't take advantage, we do this, we do that. And a lot of times, the women were the ones that must stand in that spot because often it was just them ...

Subira: "That's right."

Jennifer: "I think a lot of those things came along as; I want to say as traumas too...We have trauma from our ancestors. There's no doubt about it, from me from my perspective, it's not even a debatable point because it just comes right along with it. And I think sometimes it reminds me of the story about, why did Thanksgiving and asking why grandma cut the ends of her ham off? Eventually to find it is to fit it in the pan. And in a monkey see, monkey do, follow tradition kind of way. That part of the meal preparation was handed down, only it no longer serves as the circumstances have changed. Whereas, I believe that a lot of what comes, what people claim to believe, is with us, each of us from wherever our respective home may be. There are certain cultural roles or practices that we are just like cattle, blindly following along...And so many don't even know why the hell they do it nor do they even question!

Subira: "Rightttt. And it doesn't even serve us. So, we don't really look at it. And sometimes I think, because women are... So, like you said, we're doing it all and doing turn and flips in our heels that we don't have the luxury of time. Of quiet, peaceful, serene time, where you're not having to move, and you can just be one with yourself and go. Whoa, why am I doing that?"

Jennifer: "I think that's by design as well. I think on one level, that situation was created so that women didn't have time to stop and think and put it together and revolt, in some ways. Because "I cannot control you" if I don't have you doing what you do now, that sounds like really out there. However, it really isn't."

Subira:" HmmMmm, it's not to me."

Jennifer: "The other thing about that is, with us not choosing to take that time because it is just plain scary. Because if I sit with myself and I really stopped to go inward and touch that place in me that says, "You are behaving on the outside, something that is not even who you are. Now, I don't know who the hell you are? However, that ain't it." So, it's that whole thing inside of you or spirit inside of you says, "Look, this ain't its sister.

This is not what or who you are or what you are here to do."

"And so, if I quiet myself enough and I hear that, then I must do something about it. If I don't hear it, then I can just tootle along on my merry way and be what everyone else thinks I'm supposed to be. Sometimes, we think that is much easier, until it isn't.

Subira: "With that said; having to be responsible. Literally being 'able to respond' to yourself and your own inner urgings."

Jennifer: "Absolutely. Well, and let's be honest, that first level of consciousness is victim to responsible. So, if I don't go there with myself and my life doesn't look the way I want it to, then I get to play victim.

Subira: "Yes."

Jennifer: "So when I played victim and it's 'blame, shame and justify' then while I don't get that life either, I don't have to take responsibility for this one."

Subira: "Mmm, powerful. Powerful. I can't wait to attend one of your workshops."

Jennifer: "Thank you. It is an immersion event for sure."

"I just love bossy women. I could be around them all day. To me, bossy is not a pejorative term at all. It means somebody's passionate and engaged and ambitious and doesn't mind leading."

- Amy Poehler

CHAPTER 9

WE ARE WOMEN HEAR US ROAR

Subira: "I think you also answered my next question, which was "How does that hurt them?"

Jennifer:" Oh, for sure."

Subira: "Yes, thank you for expanding on that one. So, what's available, if they choose to practice? If women choose to practice vulnerability in their life, what's available?"

Jennifer: "Well, the simple answer is, 'Anything'. The very simple and generalized answer. What becomes available from choosing vulnerability is: One- a true relationship with themselves. Because if I am being honest and vulnerable with you than I have to be with myself. Because vulnerable doesn't come from anywhere except underneath all of that. So, choosing vulnerable means, when I first started practicing; And it literally is a practice. If it is not in your nature, that's not how you have lived your whole life you must practice it.

It will become an actual choice in the beginning for sure. And I was super resistant it was so uncomfortable, my stomach hurt, my hands were sweating, my mouth was watering, and then it would be all dry.

So, this is what I was told; "Send your significant other, my husband now though at this time we weren't married, send him a text with five reasons, the five top reasons, that you love him." Just send it to him. I'm like, Oh No, no, no, no, no. What in the hell are you people attempting to do here? And that sounds crazy right, except it really doesn't. It's like, "Oh no, because if I tell him all of that, then he's going to think that he can get away with shit that I don't put up with, or he's going to use it all against me. All of the things from my past that I brought with me or my childhood when all of those subconscious programs are created in the first place, and practicing vulnerable was a huge, huge... risk for me.

Oh, by the way, I didn't practice vulnerability with women either. So, I didn't have girlfriends that I was close to, because I couldn't trust them, blah blah blah, and all the crap that comes along with that and add to that I can only be friends with so many men before they get ridiculous. So, I often was without having the balance created through women friends. Through this process, I reconnected with a friend of mine, and she... Oh my gosh, I cannot even imagine what my life would look like today if I didn't have her. I just am not able to fathom it. I wouldn't be who I am sitting here, I know that. Because...Well, Julie kept me from out loud, saying things that I would have regretted. And would have said before, I just would have told them exactly how it was. It's not that I'm not still capable, I am. However, it wasn't going to serve me, and while before I didn't care or at least acted as if I didn't and was willing to take the consequences of that. And it's the unforeseen consequences that you don't get to choose that jump up and bite you in the ass."

Subira: "Mmm, whoooo! Yeah, you are dropping some nuggets in this book, wow!

Okay, so what would benefit women in their journey to purposeful living now that they have this information, about the power of vulnerability?"

Jennifer: "Well, what would serve them? What would benefit them? My perspective is to actually, truly choose a practice of vulnerability. In the beginning, if vulnerability is as uncomfortable for you, as it was for me. Then what I would say is choose a practice of vulnerability.

And if that means the first thing, like I would not even leave my house without my hair done, my makeup on, dressed up in an outfit. I didn't have on jeans and a t-shirt. Don't get me wrong, that was an armor for me. That kept me from being vulnerable. And that's how some women play. And other women play, "You know what, I'm not doing my hair, not wearing make-up, you can't make me be a part of that feminine", whatever it is. We're all still playing. Whichever way we choose from.

And we go through that. We work on that too 'Games of Life'.

Like, what's the game and what are the rules and are they your rules? And are you playing by these rules and those rules... Do you even want too?... What we were just talking about a minute ago? And that would be the next thing that I would do is stop and get honest with yourself. Really gut level honest. It's uncomfortable and in some ways it's super scary. And I would do it with someone that has either been there before so that they know or someone you can... I don't want to call you a "vulnerability buddy". However, someone that you have in your life that you can share that with... Because you will encounter things about yourself or things you've chosen or not chosen, and it's pretty intense. It's just that you'll have an emotional reaction, and it's a good thing. It's just I want you to be safe and responsible on this journey.

I would ask myself, "How did I come to this? What is my ``why"? So many people do things out of some misguided obligation or loyalty and they're miserable. Yet they go to school, they get a job, they do this, they do that, three kids in and all of a sudden then they're like, "This? This is my life?" I'm bored, I'm this, I'm that...Because they were never honest with themselves to figure out who they really are in there. Just following along with what was expected, what was the script that you were given."

Subira: "Yeah, and let's look at the flip side of that. What would someone do when, even with this knowledge of vulnerability, they find themselves back in old behavior patterns?"

Jennifer: "Yeah, that's one of the reasons that we really need each other. Because even the most diligent of us get hooked right back in at one time or another... And believe me, I can go on to attest to that fight of it too. And we need our women, we women need other women. And by that we need the ones that we trust, that are willing to hold us accountable, and say the hard stuff that we were talking about. The ones that know when you speak from your true essence, about your vision and what you want and then they know when your bullshit fires; and when you come at them with something completely different, they know that that's not you. They will hold you to what it was that you asked for it to begin with. Instead of going back to that old scripting and belief systems and play this role, because your parents said this, or society says that, or whatever. So, I would say that is what they really, really need, is that tribe. That tribe of women that will hold them up when they can't stand, especially in their own truth."

Subira: "Kind of like what you were talking about at the beginning about, for those people who saw Wonder Woman, right? That island. They defended each other, they trained each other, they all of that good stuff. They got strong and powerful together and all of that. Those, all of us women need to have our other wonder women, women who know I am a wonderful woman. I'm strong. I'm capable. I can also be vulnerable and tender."

Jennifer: "Yes, yes, 1000x yes."

Subira: "And I can call you on your shit, and I can also be the softest place for you to land when you're having a tough time."

Jennifer: "Oh, absolutely. I'm like your safe place because it's just necessary. I know it's also one of the things that I started doing to practice and do now because it makes my face smile and my heart warm. That is, I give honest compliments to women I don't know. Like if I am standing in line at the grocery store, and this woman has got this awesome necklace with her outfit, I'm just like, "I know you know, but that necklace amazing!" Not from a... I'm just doing it to be doing it. I would never tell them something that wasn't honest though, I love to do it.

Because I remember, my husband and I, we actually went to the horse races and I was standing there and this woman, probably about my age, was bringing, I'm going to assume her mother possibly your grandmother, but into the restroom. And the elderly woman had obviously dressed to go out and she had the coolest little, I want to say sequined, little pillbox hat, and it was so awesome! In my head I thought - that is fantastic! And so, I just leaned over and I said, "Ma'am that hat is to die for!" I mean I'm telling you Subira, her face lit up! And the daughter, who was with her, she just looked at me and she said, "Thank you."

I'm thinking, "Do you know it's simple, it's so very simple to make a positive difference in somebody else's life? It's simple." And I can promise you I got more out of that than they did. It's just so simple. So yes, do those things to have your people and be kind and gentle. I had somebody tell me, "Oh my gosh, you're so gentle" and I'm like really now? Because gentle is not ever a word that someone would have used to describe me back in the day. I'm telling you, in the grand scheme of things that day wasn't that long ago.

Subira: "I experienced you as very tender."

Jennifer: "I appreciate that."

Subira: "That's the word that I would use. That's what I would say, I experienced... She was very tender. Yeah, definitely."

"If you do not run your subconscious mind yourself, someone else will run it for you."

— Florence Scovel Shinn

CHAPTER 10

MY 4-YEAR OLD SELF IS CHOOSING WHAT?

Jennifer: "I think that if we go out into the world and treat others the way we want to be treated, just follow that golden rule that had we learned it and put it into practice in kindergarten might have helped us all a little bit, we can change the world. Just be kind. And if you won't be kind, then be silent, don't say anything."

Subira: "Yeah, yeah, yeah, wow. So, the answers to the last question about vulnerability, really seem to lend themselves to the concept of self-acceptance, what I think you believe is also an area that women could benefit from a better understanding. So, so I would like you to talk to us a little bit about what is the most common myths and or misconception that women have about self-acceptance."

Jennifer: "In my experience with my clients and students when they come in and say "I'm focused on acceptance of myself or acceptance in general, however they want to word it, it's not the same as self-worth or self-esteem. We often times get those things confused as well. However, what happens is they have a belief that something they have done or something that may have been done to them; and any of these things can range from the uncomfortable to the absolutely horrific. They, instead of coming from an understanding or perspective of those are things that happened, they are events, they are experiences. Not even speaking to fair or right or wrong. They do not define you as a human being.

They are just things that either you did or that happened to you. They're just events, they're just behavior, you cannot change any of them from the past. Nevertheless, not one of us are the same person today as we were the day that we arrived. We all change, we all evolve. And what happens is, in my experience, women get themselves caught up. Especially since, once again, we're back to that societal stuff. The inundation of, "You have to weigh a buck 02" even if you're seven-foot-tall, and you must have a long blonde hair and fingernails or whatever it is. You must drive this vehicle, and you must get this guy, or do this or do that, all that gets inundated into your sight into who you think you are from a very small age. A very small age, because most of us are not equipped with the kind of information or tools that we need to understand and battle the limiting beliefs that we all carry with us. We all carry limiting beliefs. The subconscious; and that's one of the reasons I love to work with hypnosis to bring this in; is because our subconscious beliefs about ourselves 50% of who we think we are, other people are, and the world. Fifty percent of our subconscious beliefs, we have already created by the time we are four."

Subira: "Four?!!!

Jennifer: "Four. Four years old, okay, then given another four years and by the time you're eight, there's another 30% of that, that has already been decided and embedded. So, there it is. So, 80% of who I think I am, I decided subconsciously, by eight or younger. By eight or younger, by 18 there's another 15% that's 95% and you get 5% to play with after your 18. Maybe?"

Subira: "Well, now, how does somebody break that calcification?"

Jennifer: "Yes, it means my eight-year-old balances my damn check book.

Subira: "That is so crazyyyyyy!!(laughing) Whatttt???!!"
Jennifer: "So that's why those limiting beliefs... You've heard of the power of "I AM" statements and it is very important. What I tell myself about myself is true, because it's in here and my subconscious has created. Let's say that there was something that happened when I was a kid and my mom was on the phone and I was off making a mud pie or whatever. So, I bring her in and I'm like... "Mom, mom, look, look what I made." And at first, she says, "Oh Jen, it's so cute. I love you, that's awesome, go ahead and play." So, she goes back on the phone. I'm like "Oh, so let make another one." So, I go make another mud pie the next day and I comeback in, and I've got mud and crap all over the place. I'm so excited, she's on the phone and she's like, "Okay, alright, yeah, that's awesome. Good job" and sends me on my way.

We do that a few times, but one time I come in and there have been other things that have happened where I may have questions or I've watched her or heard her; however, this time, because it has not been so loving and upbeat as the first few, I am going to be looking for evidence.

And so, I come in with the mud pie, moms on the phone, she may be having something going on, and who knows what right? Because this little four-year-old, doesn't have any idea. And she's like "JENNIFER, I AM ON THE PHONE!" I'm like "Ohh..." And so, even when she comes back and says, "Sweetheart, I shouldn't have yelled at you." and this that and the other. Does that change things on the top level? Sure, but down here where I am, like I'm either "un-lovable" or I am "not creative". That one, people have that one everywhere, people get that, "Not creative" one, someone usually it's teacher at a young age, didn't approve of your "hand turkey" or your self-portrait with arms sprouting from your huge head, right? You know what I'm talking about?

Subira: (laughing) "I do, I do.)

Jennifer: "And now all of a sudden I'm not an artist, I'm not a musician, I don't sing well. That was mine. When I was a kid. I loved to sing, I loved to sing and then somewhere in there, somebody was like, "Oh, how awful" and so now, if somebody were like... "Get up and sing" I'm like "ummm, ehhh, no." Although I've done it since then. I have been known to sing Karaoke on occasion."

Subira: (laughing) "You do karaoke."

Jennifer: "Ha-ha, yes. However, that was a thing I had told myself because somebody elssaid that. So here, I am this little kid, mom yells at me and now I think I'm not lovable, or, I'm not good enough, or I'm not enough and that then; as my subconscious job is to keep me safe. So, if it's keeping me safe and it's going to continue to put me in situations that prove me right. Because it has decided that I'm not lovable.

So, who do you think I'm going to be hooked up with then? Over and over?"

Subira: "Mmmmhmmm."

Jennifer: "And that is as an adult, and it just stays with us. It's real. And so, there are things, and it's not a hopeless situation. Believe me, there are things that we can do to uncover what your particular limiting beliefs are based on all of that. Which is what I get the blessing of being able to do as a profession. I get to work with people to find out who they are and what they want to be. It's really exciting! Because I had a 60-year-old client, who was like, "I get to decide what I want to be when I grow up!" I'm like "Yep, you sure do!"

Subira: "Niceeee."

Jennifer: "That was earlier when we were talking about that and getting with your inner child. The other thing I would do is ask yourself why you chose that? A lot of people with anything, have done it because that's what we've always had. That is one of the things that are like fingernails on a chalkboard to me.

"Oh, so why are you choosing that? How did you come to that decision?" "Well it's what we've always done." "Ahhh really…okay?" And so that just permeates through our culture too."

"Do what you feel in your heart to be right, for you'll be criticized anyway. You'll be damned if you do, and damned if you don't"

- Eleanor Roosevelt

CHAPTER 11

DAMNED IF YOU DO, DAMNED IF YOU DON'T

Subira: "Right. Whoooo. So, what's another area or concept that's often swirled in this myth and misconception that women have about living an intentional life of purpose? Because I don't think most women live intentionally. I think it's like you said, they're operating on scripts that have been written... And I don't know... I'd like to hear from you about what else is kind of swirled up in there with that.

Jennifer: "Yeah, absolutely, I would agree with you that most women don't live intentionally. A lot of time, they don't even understand what that means. The concept of doing something by intention, having it happen, is foreign in their experience. A lot of that can be attributed to the fact that women tend to stuff their voices and if they even understand what their vision is that will pull them forward, they stuff all of that down. Based on many things, though most of it is going to be shame and guilt. Which is from the inside out, it eats you up from the inside out. There is a difference between guilt and shame. A lot of times people think it's the same, or it doesn't matter what the difference is. And the truth is, it matters, it truly matters.

Subira: "MmmHmmm."

Jennifer: "Brenè Brown is like my favorite right?"

Subira: "I love her too!"

Jennifer: "Okay, so I love her, I am like her biggest fan. I'm not like stalker, level yet, however, I just think that what she does and her willingness to share it with the world, is a huge gift to the rest of us.

Subira: "MmmHmmm."

Jennifer: "Which is why I know she's following her true essence and it beams right out of her. It's just very exciting. I think she's amazing. Her definitions are very workable definitions for myself and the women that I work with. And guilt is "I did something bad. "So 'bad' for lack of a better word, if we are in a judgement, of one over the other. So "I did something bad." And then shame, is the same event, but my perception isn't that "I did something bad" or my "behavior was bad" shame is, "I am bad."

Subira: "Ohhh, meaning my personage "is bad".

Jennifer: "Yes."

Subira: "Who I am as a human being, who I am as a woman is "bad."

Jennifer: "Yes."

Subira: "Well, ya know, we can even take that a little bit further when not all of us, but at least most in the Western world, but let's look at little girls. And let's go back to what you just said about how at four years old we're 50%, we know who we are, supposedly, at least had subconsciously decided."

Jennifer: "Right."

Subira: "50% it's already programmed. The programming is in effect. Well, so you've got these little girls at four years old going to church, and whatever, denomination or synagogue or wherever they go. And the overarching storyline there is, "You're a sinner""

Jennifer: "MmmHmm, just by being here."

Subira: So, my God, of course, "I'm bad, of course, everything I do is bad." And so, these women are walking around and men too... But we're talking about women here. And literally marinating in.... Imagine a shirt that you're tye-dying or something, and you just dunk it and you lift, and you dunk it and you lift it and it's in the shame over and over and... Oh, oh my gosh..."

Jennifer: "Yessss, yesss."

Subira: "I'm so grateful. that you do the work that you do."

Jennifer: "Thank you. I really do think that I am the one that's blessed. And what I have learned, experienced, witnessed with the shame we were talking about earlier and wearing that shame like it's a scarlet letter. It becomes interesting to me that you brought up the religious aspect. Because I remember that as part of my childhood. I was going to be doing a dance recital. I was in, likely, first grade and my Mom had laid all my stuff out and I was sleeping, and I was just too excited! I woke up and I put on my outfit, and then of course, I got tired and went back to sleep in my dance clothes, that I was supposed to wear to dance in on stage. Mom comes in to wake me up, and she says, "Jennifer Dayle! I can't believe you! What have you got on? What are you doing?"... And in my head, what 6 or 7 -year old Jennifer is thinking was "Once again, I am in trouble and the devil made me do it, so I don't understand why I am in trouble? When I was told in Sunday school...etc. etc." Do you know what I mean, that was my perception? I was so taken aback that you told me I am good and that it's the devil who is bad AND I had her the phrase "The Devil made me do it" so many times. Then I thought, "Well shit, I don't understand. Well, I doubt I thought "Well shit" though it's possible, and now all I do is get in trouble."

Subira: "I am damned if I do, and I am damned if I don't! Literally!"

Jennifer: "Yes! Yes, and so the concept of shame and its effect, is interesting because research has shown that with people who have substance use dependencies, challenges and whatnot. That the correlation of shame and addiction, the cause and effect so to speak, they are unable to distinguish which came first - was shame first so the effect was drug use or was drug use first which created the shame? So, I another Brenè Brown piece of info is that, I think what she said was 'An addict needs shame, like a man dying of thirst needs saltwater."

Subira: "Wow."

Jennifer: "Yes. Because as I am sure most know, saltwater will kill a dehydrated person. So, is that it's just this whole heavy weight of wearing, you hear that, that expression "You're wearing the weight of the world on your shoulders." That didn't come from nowhere. We can physically see people who are really in shame, shrink. Like their attempting to disappear, they shrink, because it's so painful and heavy."

Subira: "Yeah."

Jennifer: "Some of it is, well, it's all in the process. That's the interesting thing too, you and I could have the same experience and yet there's no way to say this experience creates this thought process because we're all different and do things and perceive things and process them differently. We know that it is based on an emotionally and/or repetitive event, though who will process it how is not something that can be 100% pinpointed. Only likelihoods or percentages. So, we have to be super careful because our teachers do it to our children."

Subira: "Well."

Jennifer: "And no, I don't think it's usually on purpose. Though there's not enough education about what it is to be on this undefined journey as a human versus a roadmap to give you answers and direct that if you just say this, then they'll do this. However, I don't want to get on a soap box on that one ..."

Subira: "Well, hey ...I've talked to very few other women in this field who have been willing to share from such a place of vulnerability, not to be cliché, but you really, really are and it's refreshing.

Jennifer: "Thank you."

Subira: "It's refreshing because you think if someone were just to take a snapshot and look at you... You have this short-cropped, bleached blonde hair, your whole sleeve tattoo going on, your background, and all, but you are this really...You are the embodiment of vulnerability and tenderness. And I have come to truly appreciate it. Before this interview but, especially now."

Jennifer: "Thank you, that makes my heart smile. I promise you, 20 years ago, that would likely not have been your impression of me. So, it's proof positive that transformation is possible."

"Spiritual growth involves giving up the stories of your past so the universe can write a new one."

\- Marianne Williamson

Chapter 12
Choose & Move

Subira: "MmmmHmmm. Just be around a circle of other healers it's amazing, simply amazing. Now that you have exposed some of the limiting beliefs that tend to affect women collectively. I think it's important to also tune into what will empower women who embrace that we are connected. That every woman has not only Divine purpose but is actually the Divine embodied in her femininity. That piece of this conversation was powerful. I would love to dive there a little bit more, especially later we could do a whole other conversation around just that.

Jennifer: "Yeah, that'd be great. I would suggest in connection with those two things: First is action. You must choose and move."

Subira: "Ok."

Jennifer: "It's an interesting thing because women are doers. That is how we are put together. It is how we make our way through the world. Men are not doers, though they will still take action. And so, you have to be very careful about how you understand what I say. When I say action is necessary. Not just to be "busy do". That's not what I'm talking about, what I'm talking about is that place where you have set a goal, a true goal not just a want or wish and your thought is, "This is my outcome. I am reaching this." Then I don't care if you know what to do or don't know what to do, it doesn't matter, do something. Because as you set that intention and you move forward, "the how" ... the way to your goal, is none of your business. It doesn't matter. The Universe will provide that to you. What you must do is choose and move.

The other thing that is just as, if not more, paramount, is the care of self. Women are not necessarily good at caring for themselves. I am not speaking to the ability to function independently, nor just massages and scented candles. I mean, the norm for most (and the accepted societal norm for most of the planet) is for women to care for everyone else, often to their own detriment. However, self-care is a necessity, a gift and from my perspective, an obligation. It is a gift to you and others. You are a part of the Universe, you are Connected, you are Divine. I don't say that lightly. It is, if you will choose to stop and really contemplate what I'm saying, the piece you must acknowledge to find your purpose. You are Divine. Therefore, please care for that body that you're in because it's what is home to you on this journey. To be able to find that purpose and be in alignment and service of others I must care for myself as I am unable to give more than I have. I certainly can't give to you from an empty vessel. Which I have personally experienced, believe me, I subscribed to the I must do, do, do to exhaustion to prove my worth, etc. etc. And what do you have on the inside, nothing because if you are not nourishing and growing yourself...you are in decay whether physically, mentally, emotionally or spiritually. Or all of the above most likely. Please, if that has also been part of your journey, be gentle and kind with yourself. You have been doing the best that you can with the information you had. This is so often a journey to accepting one's worth. And I do mean accepting...your worth is your birthright.

Without that acceptance, something has to be found to attempt to fill it up. That's often when drugs and alcohol, sex, shopping, eating, gambling, whatever it is one chooses in an attempt to fill that void or chase for worthiness.

Subira: "But when you can... And it's like you said, you have to work on yourself first and have that safe support so that you can kind of practice. But oh my gosh, it's rigged in our favor. That's what I hear you saying."

Jennifer: "Absolutely, it is. We designed it that way. It goes back to the first three levels of consciousness we were talking about before. It's our conscious mind, we get the five senses in there, we make decisions based on what we know consciously. However, that subconscious stuff is where your emotions are and where your programs are and some of your programs really work for you to provide desired results. If you have a program that says "you cannot go to sleep until your teeth are brushed" your dentist bill, as you get to be my age is not going to look like mine did. You can have programs that provide results you want and ones you do not.

The Superconscious we were talking about where all is connected... That's the Divine, the Universe, God, whatever name you choose to refer to it, is what holds us all and its job is to provide. So, if one will accept their worth and be... And yes, I definitely mean "Be" as in "be-do-have" not "do-have-be" If I "be" who I am and who I am is a worthy, connected, Divine being and I help the women next to me? Why would the Divine then turn around and not provide? That's it's job, to provide."

Subira: "Ladies, I hope you just got that. She just gave us the formulaaaaa. (laughing) That's' beautiful."

Jennifer: "That it is."

"I am a vulnerable, feminine, worthy goddess fully accepting my radiant and divine beauty. Moment by moment sharing my authentic, highly charged spirit with the world."

-fth

CHAPTER 13

#FEMININEGRACE

Subira: "Is there anything else Jennifer, that I haven't asked you about myths and misconceptions about transformation, about vulnerability as it relates to women that you'd like to share?"

Jennifer: "Okay, well, as much as I think I might just shut up on that last one because it was a bit more palatable information. There is a very real situation that's happening in the world today for women and it has happened for years and years and years. So, question to you. Hormones are real? They exist, right?"

Subira: "Right."

Jennifer: "And women have the memory loss and hormonal storms and crying spells and all those things that come from them?"

Subira: "Yeah, all of that is true."

Jennifer: "And while some of the times we say some

of that stuff a little "tongue in-cheek". It is part of the female experience, it's part of who we are. It is Divine and there is purpose to it. Then add to that, we have an underlying acceptance and adherence of misogyny in our society.

So, we don't talk about it, that's taboo. We certainly don't talk about it in front of men or in public! Hell, we don't even talk about it to each other, we just don't talk about it. So then by the time women become my age and have experiences where thinking the mind has gone becomes recurrent. And there has been no conversation, education, even commiseration, it is frightening. No frame of reference, no logical explanation. Only persistent judgment, especially from within because you are terrified to ask any questions or talk of your incidents for fear you really are losing your mind.

Then, when you can no longer take it, no longer laugh it off or explain it away with plausibles that are socially acceptable, and you muster the courage to talk and ask questions... there's judgment from outside that comes back at you. Or when it's something that you obviously have no control over, my memory lapses, and sometimes it is impossible to focus. It also has been used to disqualify women from professions and jobs because we're too emotional, or it has been turned into a derogatory term or used derogatorily toward women or to describe women.

And that has become just standard misogyny in society. Heaven forbid I stand up for myself. Then it becomes... "Oh, well, she's bitchy... She must be on the rag, blah, blah, blah.

It becomes a way to just brush women away and

under the rug because anything she had to say was obviously, ridiculous because she doesn't, she can't even control herself."

Subira: "Mmmhmm."

Jennifer: "I have had several fights within myself in those arenas, simply growing up with my story and it is a story, we all have them.   However, my story was female=defective/male=better and spawning from that (along with the cementing of it by my third-grade teacher Mrs. Taylor) damned if I do, damned if I don't.

So, I would always fight for my space, to prove my worth, no matter whether it was a male-dominated situation wasn't a requirement, though it was a bonus as far as my programs were concerned. I'm not sure when I became truly aware that it was way more than being competitive and I was "proving", theoretically, that I can do anything better. That being male wasn't the end all/be all and that I had been worth being born. Usually big and loud and public, wanting everyone to see me and have witnesses to my "proving" my worth, earning my right to exist... and if it had to be toe- to- toe with you, all the better." Which also kept people at a distance who may be able to see through my facade and confirm I was defective."

Subira: "Yeah."

Jennifer: "That's not the place for me to come from today. However, there are just as many women who accept misogyny as truth, as there are men. And that's the part that I really want to get to in this little blurb that I'm sharing with you right now. The message to each woman is that they, women, can embrace each part of themselves and love ourselves at each stage of our journey. And please, please, share your experience to the benefit of everyone. Because while I'm over here thinking I'm a crazy person, not understanding what is happening to me, having to defend myself to people who want to point it out as detrimental and having no information/ammunition to fight back.

Subira: "Yeah, just hysteria, right?"

Jennifer: "They used to put you in the hospital for that!! Female hysteria! What in the actual hell?"

Subira: "Mmmhmmmm."

Jennifer: "If ladies who had been through this prior to me had shared their experience mine would likely have been (still be) more acceptable and less scary. From my understanding, they actually used to... I read this book, which was actually an inspiration for some of the content in my Women's Empowerment seminar. It is set in an era when tribal and nomadic living were a common lifestyle. However, the women of this culture, and this was back, well it actually tells a story that is in the Bible. Though, this story gets told from the perspective of one of the young girls, and it's fascinating!"

Subira: "What is it called?"

Jennifer: "It's called the *Red Tent*. It's this fascinating journey of woman, of bonding, of ritual, of sisterhood. They're talking about what it means to honor the goddess within and to bring forth what that means to them.

Subira: "Wow!"

Jennifer: "Truly what it means for yourself in the world. It's a big responsibility to be Woman. And I don't mean that like "Oh God, here you go. I'm going to give you something else to take on to prove your worth" ...I mean that we are the Creators. We are the continuation of humanity. So, if we do not honor that within ourselves and each other, then we cannot enroll anyone else to honor it, either.

So, it always starts with self. No matter how cliché it may sound, it does start with me. I must honor the feminine in me and love and embrace her, both the intensity of her power and the softness of her gracious heart and be able to express that from a place of creation and love. Embrace the wholeness that is Woman and Goddess And then do the same for the other women in my life, so that we can let that be our legacy. Not that we tear one another down, exploit or expunge femininity, fight for less than we deserve and abandon our Divine Goddess and Sisterhood. That's not the legacy as a woman I want to leave my children or my grandchildren. I want them, I have two daughters and I want them to stand in Woman proudly, confidently, and loving themselves and knowing that. I have a grandson who is five and I want him to love and respect femininity, understand cherishing the women in his life and have the ability to own his masculinity without degrading himself or anyone else because toxic masculinity is permeating the globe now. Though, that is definitely a subject for another time.

So, perhaps a longer answer than you bargained for, that's the other thing that I think is wrapped around all of that."

Subira: "Wow. You are amazing. I am so fortunate and so blessed to be able to sit in this seat of receptivity and hear your wisdom, so thank you so much for sharing this, thank you for agreeing to this interview. Thank you for sharing your experience and I am just blown away right now."

Jennifer: "Thank you for creating the space for this to occur. I feel privileged."

Subira: "I'm so looking forward to… (tearing up) This wasn't part of the interview...Wow, I'm just so blown away. Okay, so officially thank you so much Jennifer King Brogan for sharing your expertise, your experience, your love and your wisdom, your Divine Feminine wisdom. I think if I were to boil all of this down, that is really what it comes to. I saw the Goddess that you are. The Creatrix, that you are. And thank you, that you for reminding me of who I am."

Jennifer: "Thank you, Subira, the pleasure has been all mine"

Contact Information & Upcoming Events

If you wish to contact the author:
nakedwithmyclotheson@gmail.com
elevatepublishingllc@gmail.com

Schedule appointments:
https://calendly.com/jkbrogan-hypno-coach

Website (under construction):
www.nakedwithmyclotheson.com and
www.elevateunow.net

Facebook:
www.facebook.com/ExposeExpandElevate

Come join us! Email for dates!!

Level One:

3-day Workshop: EXPOSE!

EXPOSE! is a 30-hour EDUCATIONAL workshop on
PERSONAL EXPLORATION and DISCOVERY exposing
YOUR true POTENTIAL allowing you the opportunity to
begin the journey to LEADERSHIP, AWARENESS, & the
ABILILTY to create results NOW!

#chooseu; #umatter; #goddess; #femininegrace;
#getnaked; #jenniferkingbrogan; #jdkbrogan;

Made in the USA
Middletown, DE
16 February 2020